**Also by Bob Hartman:**
*The Busy Builders*
*Bob Hartman's Rhyming Bible*
*The Link-it-Up Bible*
*The Tell-it-Together Gospel*

*The Lion Storyteller Bible 25th Anniversary Edition*
*Welcome to the Journey*
*Where Do I Come from?*

**Forthcoming:**
*Bob Hartman's Rhyming Christmas*
*The Fantastic Feast*
*One Sheep Short*

————————

**The original version of this story is found in the Gospel of Matthew, where Jesus says:**
'Anyone who listens to my teaching and follows it is wise, like a person who builds a house on solid rock. Though the rain comes and the winds beat against that house, it won't collapse because it is built on bedrock. But anyone who hears my teaching and doesn't obey it is foolish, like a person who builds a house on sand. When the rains come and the winds beat against that house, it will collapse with a mighty crash.'
**Matthew 7.24–27** (New Living Translation)

————————

First published in Great Britain in 2021

Society for Promoting Christian Knowledge
36 Causton Street, London SW1P 4ST
www.spck.org.uk

Text copyright © Bob Hartman 2021
Illustrations copyright © Mark Beech 2021

*British Library Cataloguing-in-Publication Data*
A catalogue record for this book is avaliable from the British Library

ISBN 978–0–281–08508–8

Printed by Imago

Produced on paper from sustainable forests

# Bob Hartman

# THE BUSY BUILDERS

Fantastic illustrations by
## Mark Beech

A builder went to build a house,
a happy, homey kind of house,

so he dug down,

dug down,

dug down deep.

4

Yes, he dug down,

dug down,

dug down deep.

5

He shovelled hard,
the work was tough

he moved the dirt,
he huffed and puffed

and he dug down,

dug down,

dug down deep.

Yes, he dug down,

dug down,

dug down deep.

And then, in time, he hit a rock,
a great big chunky house-sized block,

and he dug down,

dug down,

dug down deep.

Yes, he dug down,

dug down,

dug down deep.

And on that rock he built his walls
brick and stone stacked thick and tall

and he dug down,

dug down,

dug down deep.

Yes, he dug down,

dug down,

dug down deep.

And in those walls stacked thick and tall,
he built his ceilings, rooms and halls

and he dug down,

dug down, dug down deep.

Yes, he dug down,

dug down,

dug down deep.

11

And on those walls stacked thick and tall
he built a roof above it all

So when the storms came crashing down

and when the floods came rushing round

the house stood firm upon
that ground

for he dug down, dug down, dug down deep.
Yes, he dug down,
dug down,
dug down deep.

15

Another builder went to build
a happy, homey kind of house,

but he never dug down,

dug down deep.

No he never dug down,

dug down deep.

17

He left his shovel in the shed.

He left his pick behind the bed

and he never dug down,
dug down deep.

No he never dug down,
dug down deep.

Too tricky or too far below?
Too heavy or too hard, who knows?

But he never dug down,

dug down deep.

No he never dug down,

dug down deep.

He never found that rock at all
so on the clay he built his walls

for he never dug down,

dug down deep.

No he never dug down,

dug down deep.

Because the clay could hold no weight
the walls he built would not stand straight

The rooms inside
were kinda wonky

crooked like a
leg o' donkey

24

for he never dug down, dug down deep.

No he never dug down, dug down deep.

25

And when he put the roof on top
it looked like the whole thing might flop

for he never dug down,

dug down deep.

No he never dug down,

dug down deep.

26

So when the storms
came crashing down

and when the floods
came rushing round

28

that house fell flat on to the ground.

For he never dug down,
dug down deep.

No, he never dug down,
dug down deep.

'So those who hear the words I say,'
said Jesus, 'and who don't obey,
are like the man who built on clay,
whose house fell to the ground that day.

For he never dug down,

dug down deep.

No, he never dug down,

dug down deep.'

'But those who hear the words I say,'
said Jesus, 'and those words obey,
are like the man who chipped away
whose house stood on the rock that day.

For he dug down,
dug down,
dug down deep.

Yes he dug down,
dug down,
dug down deep.'